sketchy Muma

SKETCHY MUMA

Anna Lewis

Quercus

For Pops.
I made this book
for You, but You
have been the
making of me.
Love You
FOREVER
X

Contents

Two Blue Lines   7

Any News?   37

Hello Again Sofa   53

Brave New World   81

Keep on Moving   103

This is our love story.

TWO BLUE LINES

so are
you
ready?

Is anyone
ever ready?

All I know
is I want
more of you in
this world.

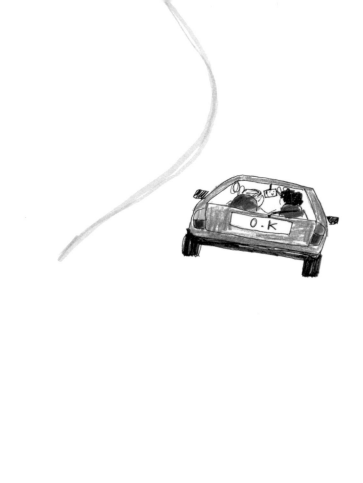

Have you tried a GINGER NUT?

I'm glad I found you.

I CAN 🖤

D R E A M.

nesting

Have you thought of any names yet?

So, for a boy I was thinking....

Don't you remember that weird boy from school called that?

He he... sounds like a washing powder!

I had a gerbil called that once.

Oh.

Womb Grooves

Don't stay
up too
late...

O.K.
Just want
to get
it all
ready.

HOW
TO BUILD
A COT.

You are the best.

Your heart
beats with
mine.

PARTY TIME!

(Third Trimester Style)

Hmm...

come on—
you know
it!

Birth Preparation – call the midwife

PUT 'EM UP RANDOM STRANGER!

Would you mind?

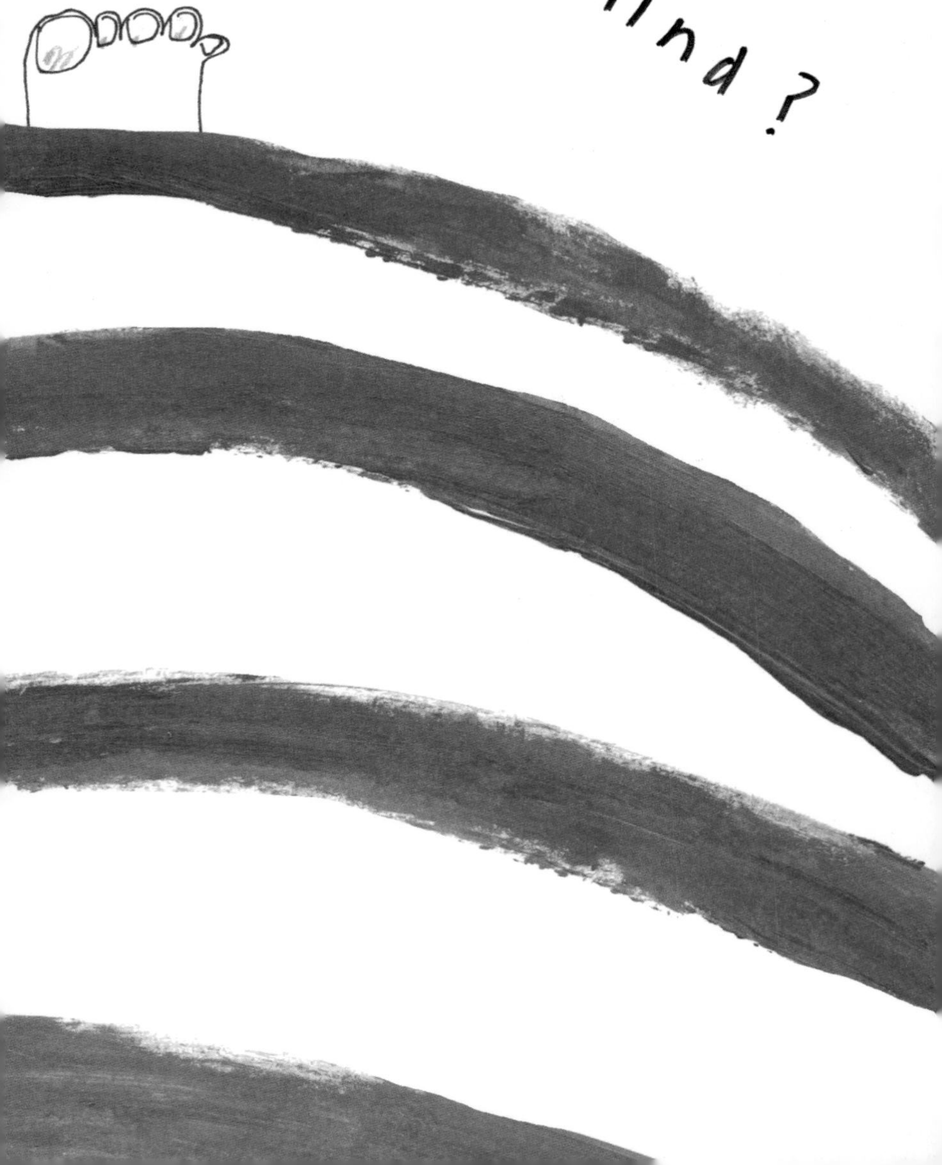

WOW YOU LOOK
ENORMOUS!
sure it's just the
one in there? You
are the size of
a HOUSE!
Absolutely HUGE
O.M.G You are
SOOOOOOO
MASSIVE

under surveillance

LAST PREGNANCY SNACK-OFF

ANY NEWS?

I'm waiting for you too.

It's probably best to test the **TENS** MACHINE <u>BEFORE</u> your partner is in Labour.

THE HOSPITAL RIDE

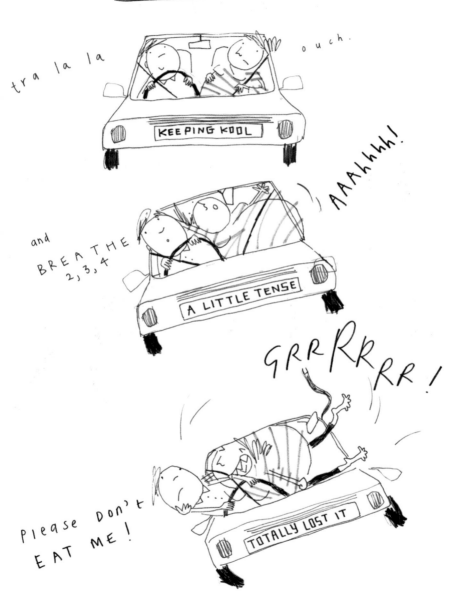

I wanted to be with you.

Thanks for coming mum

OPTIMISTIC HOSPITAL BAG

HOT gossip kim

my hot post baby body

50p

£1 £1

CAR PARK CHANGE

CHILL tunes

BLISS SCENT

RED HOT MAMA

oil de massage

ENERGIZE

KIT-KAT

EGG + CRESS

SHADES OF A BIRTHING PARTNER

FLUSTERED LOBSTER

SPEW N CHEW

WHIFF O NERVES

QUIVER N SHIVER

LEGGED IT

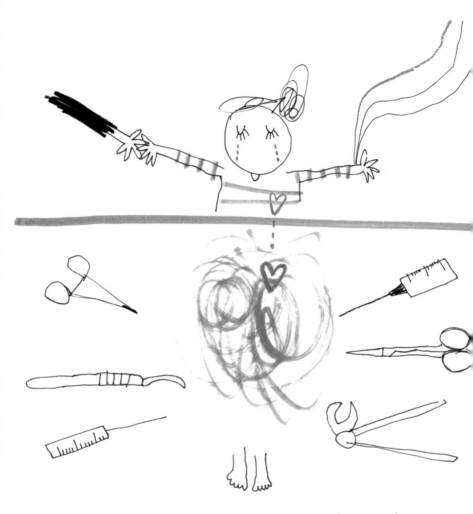

Not sure what happened next
but I know you were holding
my hand.

I did it, She is here.
I named her after you
because I LOVE you.

The hospital night

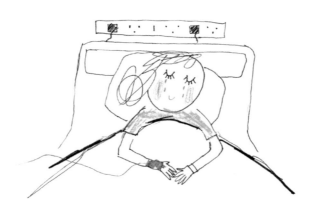

You thought I was
sleeping but I heard
You.

My beautiful girl.
You are finally here.
No words will ever
come close to how
you make me feel. ♡

A Beginner – (like every other new mum)

That's it my girl!
Mother knows best!

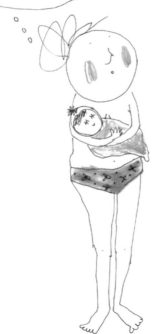

But I don't know anything yet.

Well of course it's YOU_R_ choice .....

JUST DO IT!

BREAST IS BEST

DON'T MAKE A BOOB BREAST FEED!

HURRAY FOR BREASTS!

WA
WA
WA

WOBBLY HEART ♡

So tiny and fragile.
Let's grow STRONG
together.

HELLO AGAIN SOFA

FIRST CAR JOURNEY HOME

First night home

OMG THIS IS REAL

some time later.

OMG This is Real

24 HOURS HOME

GOING SOLO

WA
WA
WA

I've put a t-bag in the cup and left you some of those biscuits you like with the choc-chips in.

Be back as soon as I can.

Love you.

I wanted to be perfect.

You are better than perfect,
you are REAL.

Subject to change.

RINSE + REPEAT ↻

WASH IT ALL AWAY
AND START AGAIN.

AHH SLEEEEP!
I WANT YOU!
I NEED YOU!
I MISS YOU!
It's not the same without you – when are you coming back?
ZZZ
ZZZ
ZZZ
ZZZ

I'D do anything to get You.

ZZZ

Really <u>Late</u> night shopping

3:06 am

answers.com | Baby sleep | 🔍

A-ZZZZ of sleep ☑ **BUY NOW**
Sweet Dream Lavender oil ☑ **BUY NOW**
White noise thingy ☑ **BUY NOW**
The sleep whisperer re-vamped ☑ **BUY NOW**
The Soothing Soother thing ☑ **BUY NOW**
Essential sleep secrets ☑ **BUY NOW**
Double Espresso coffee machine. ☑ **BUY NOW**

🛒 73 ITEMS IN YOUR BASKET.

DOMESTIC GODDESS (ish)

WA
  WA
WA

I'll try and cook something decent tomorrow night.

Yeah, no worries, I like Italian anyway.

post-Pregnancy CAPSULE WARDROBE

Hmm... think I'll go a
bit different for the
weekend and wear my
DARK black leggings rather
than my PLAIN black leggings.

wonder

I can't believe I have
just made You.

'Helping Hand'

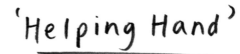

hello?
Are you still there?
So what do you think?

Ummm.... yes. What a
lovely idea to have
(insert relative) to stay for
3 months to help us 'SETTLE IN'.

So are you in a ROUTINE yet?

oh yes. I usually have one pack
of biscuits per hour.

WA WA WA

WA WA WA

WORK STUFF

My main MELT DOWN is at about six,
(with a few mini ones in between).

And my last bottle is about TEN.

Indecent Exposure

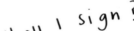

LOOK at You

You are beautiful.
All of You.

I'm going to tell you
everyday because it's true.

The world gets bigger.
Hugs get tighter.

4:00 a.m. Musings.

WA
WA
WA

hmmm. You're a tricky one 4 am. I mean 3 am, well, you still have potential, maybe four more glorious hours' sleep, well ok three, if things go to plan. But 4 am, you're heading dangerously close to 5 am and that's just nearly 6 am. Before you know it that overly cheerful bird is piping up and it's GAME OVER

OK one more round of twinkle twinkle. Let's do this.

la la la ♪♫ ♪

wind-eze

Post-labour look in Mirror

OMG! I've turned into a MR MAN!

𝓛ittle Miss what the HELL HAPPENED!

perks of the job

1 FEED =

3 cakes + ½ tub chocs
(roughly).

This is PEACE. ♡

BRAVE NEW WORLD

First Group

5.35 pm cabin Fever

Oh great you're home

Darling shall I . . . .

NO NO NO
NO NO NO
NO
and NO

WORK STUFF

WORK STUFF

It's fine. I'll nip out for MILK.

Thrill seeking in aisle

Ahhh a late night solo supermarket shop . . . . oh yes.

Just popping out
for milk ....

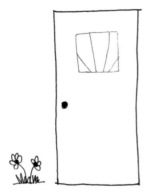

... with the baby.

I only Popped in for milk ...

SUPERMARKET
season's Greetings

OK. STAY FOCUSED. YOU ARE HERE FOR <u>ONE</u> THING.

Oh YES! LOVE it!

Ahhhh...SO CUTE

LiTTle PUD

IT'S A MUST!

Oh, I forgot the milk ...

XMAS

TEA

No. of cups attempted to drink today →

1 2 3 4 5

6 7 8 9 10

11 12 13 14 15

16 17 18 19 20

21 22 23

Best Friend

So do you fancy DRINKS Friday?

back to planet Earth sometime soon.....

in this BONKERS NEW BABY WORLD but I think I shall be coming down at the moment in a bit Um....I'm kind of a bit upside down

Friendly Advice

Oooh someone's not happy!

hmmm. What star sign you got there?

Teeth maybe?

Ummm.

Is she warm enough?

WA WA WA

WA WA WA WA

MILK

nappies

Looks a bit hungry to me

What did mummy do to you!

CHILL GUYS.

I'm a baby. Sometimes we cry, Muma is getting there!

Current Affairs

so what's your view on
the latest political debate?

Ummmm... I Agree with DADDY PIG.

channeling my inner <u>UN</u>tidiness

* I c<u>an</u> learn to live in a mess *

Every lump of play-doh in the carpet is a sign of FUN mum

* chaos is COOL! *

and 5, 4, 3, 2, 1 - open your eyes...

Ahhhh!!!
I CAN'T LIVE IN THIS MESS!!

All _PUMPED UP_ and nowhere to go.

Fresh Air.

Precious little thing.
I won't always get it right
because I am learning too.
But I hope one day you will be
as proud of me as I am of You. ♡

UP ALL NIGHT

Welcome to
Rise n Shine
COFFEE HOUSE

HI!

WA   WA
WA

XXL XL L M

6:01 AM

HI!

JUST GIVE ME THE STRONGEST
THING YOU'VE GOT IN HERE AND
EVERYONE GETS OUT ALIVE.

Be safe. You are my world.

Let's meet for COFFEE...

Mind the, No not the....

VERY HOT

OK hang on a bit

um so yeah

WIPE IT!

MILK

TOM

TOM

MAYO

RICE CAKES

SUGAR

MAYO

and not drink any of it...

back in a minute

sorry what was that?

or chat to each other...

Same time next week? Yeah, Lovely.

You are Enough

RICE CAKES RICECAKES RICE CAKES!

simple

Nothing particularly extraordinary
has happened today but we have
made a FAMILY and that is
EVERYTHING   to me. ♡

Wide World.

However far you go,
I'll never stop HOLDING You. ♡

KEEP ON MOVING

Mother Love

I would not have really noticed what they did before because it all seemed so ordinary.

But I was not looking properly.
What mothers do is
EXTRA ordinary.

So glad
you are home.

Me too.

Granny Pants v Fancy Pants

Goodbye Fancy Little knickers.
It was great while it lasted.
It's not <u>You</u> its <u>ME</u>. I've changed.
You look Fantastic and all that
but I'm looking for a bit more
long-term stability in my
knicker drawer. X

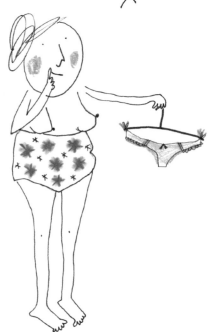

Post-Breastfeeding bra fitting

How did I get so LUCKY!

FIRST WORDS

Mmmm u u MA

mmmmm
Muuuum

Muumaaaa

Mmmmmm
Muuuum

Mmmummy

Mmmmmm
Muuuum

hey DADA how was work?

The Washing Mountain

Well, I'm determined to get on top of this washing today...

aaahhh zzzzz

and have a BIG old NAP

Where does all the LOVE go?

How can a lifetime
of love ever truly
leave us?
Maybe we
become the
Love.

I would do anything
for You.

Voice mail.

Hi mum.
It's only me.
No need to pick up.
It's getting late.
Just wanted to say
I GET IT NOW

Thankyou for your
EVERYTHING.
I Love you.

You make me
Happy Daddy ♡

Bird

I sing for you. ♡

A Good Day's Work

Crikey I'm not achieving
anything at the moment...

KEEPING
UP WITH
the TRASH

CHOC-CHIPS

Actually, hang on a minute...I have
recently created a totally unique human!
Hell that's bloody AMAZING!

Pass the biscuits...

I'm so proud of you.

Your words
mean EVERYTHING
to me dad.

SLOW DOWN

I'm not going to rush around today I'm just going to savour your little world.

LATE NAP

There will always be tea to
make but there won't always
be this. ♡

Walking Home

Let the storms
come and go.
It's o.k.
You have made
me STRONG and
BRAVE.

keep going.
I've got you.

Acknowledgements

Thank you to my brilliant agent Lauren Gardner from Bell Lomax Moreton, who found me in a sea of other voices. I feel so lucky to have found an agent who really understands me. Your dogged determination and belief in me has made this project happen and I am so grateful to you Lauren.

Thank you to Katy Follain, Jane Sturrock and all the fantastic team at Quercus, who saw a spark of something in my illustrations that has now turned into this book. With your sensitive support and nurturing guidance you have allowed me to make the type of book that can connect with other parents, yet is still very authentic to me. Thank you to Sarah Greeno too for her careful design.

Thank you to my dear friend Helen Jones for your constant support and positivity, keeping me going on my creative path. You give off the best vibes ever. XXX

Thanks to you Nic, for being with me from the very beginning, watching me hatch endless creative plans with your typical positive encouragement. Hey I pulled this one off, get the coffee machine on and the flowers ready!

Thanks Bretty for just being so incredibly kind and loyal and always, always being there.

Thanks to my family and other lovely friends who have supported me in many different ways along my path. XXX

Thanks to all my mum friends who have grown with me through this crazy first-time-motherhood ride, we have a great gang! Big hugs Claire and cheers for the laughs Nat!

The biggest thanks will always go to you Ray, how could it not? I could write a whole book on what you mean to me but there would never be enough pages because you have given me everything. I love you. XXXXX

Lastly a big thank you to all my followers on social media that support sketchy Muma. I have been so moved by the many poignant and heartfelt messages you have sent me and I am so glad my pictures reach you. All I have ever wanted to do for a job is draw and you have made this happen.

Biography

Anna Lewis is a published children's illustrator from Cornwall. Sketchy Muma became Anna's personal project whilst she was at home raising her baby, expressing her experiences of first-time motherhood through illustration, in case her daughter ever became a mum herself one day.

After sharing her illustrations on social media, Anna began to gain a following of other parents. She now receives many messages from fans who often comment on her ability to get exactly to the heart of how they feel about parenthood in such a simple and honest way.

Anna lives in St. Agnes with her filmmaker partner and their daughter.

First published in Great Britain in 2017 by

Quercus Editions Ltd
Carmelite House
50 Victoria Embankment
London EC4Y 0DZ

An Hachette UK company

A CIP catalogue record for this book is available from the British Library

HB ISBN 978 1 78648 638 7

10 9 8 7 6 5 4 3 2 1

Designed and typeset by Sarah Greeno

Printed and bound in China by 1010 Printing